DO IT

Sounds True
Boulder, CO 80306

Sounds True is a trademark of Sounds True, Inc.

Published 2020

Cover & Interior Design by
Heather Scott (More Milk Studio)

Author photo ©Lily Diamond

Excerpt from "Be Your Own Story" reprinted by
permission of the Estate of Chloe A. Morrison

Printed in South Korea

Library of Congress Cataloging-in-Publication Data
Names: Walker, Rebecca, 1969 November 17- author. |
     Diamond, Lily, author.
Title: What's your story? : a journal for everyday evolution /
     by Rebecca Walker & Lily Diamond.
Description: Boulder : Sounds True, Inc., 2020.
Identifiers: LCCN 2019056621 (print) | LCCN 2019056622
     (ebook) | ISBN 9781683643609 (paperback) | ISBN
     9781683644323 (ebook)
Subjects: LCSH: Self-realization. | Expression (Philosophy) |
     Adjustment (Psychology)
Classification: LCC BF637.S4 W348 2020 (print) | LCC BF637.
     S4 (ebook) | DDC 158.1--dc23
LC record available at https://lccn.loc.gov/2019056621
LC ebook record available at https://lccn.loc.gov/2019056622

10 9 8 7 6 5 4 3

WHAT'S

A JOURNAL FOR

YOUR

EVERYDAY EVOLUTION

STORY?

REBECCA WALKER + LILY DIAMOND

sounds true
BOULDER, COLORADO

ALSO BY

REBECCA WALKER

Black, White & Jewish: Autobiography of a Shifting Self

To Be Real: Telling the Truth and Changing the Face of Feminism

Baby Love: Choosing Motherhood After a Lifetime of Ambivalence

Adé: A Love Story

Black Cool: One Thousand Streams of Blackness

One Big Happy Family: 18 Writers Talk About Open Adoption, Mixed Marriage, Polyamory, Househusbandry, Single Motherhood, and Other Realities of Truly Modern Love

What Makes a Man: 22 Writers Imagine the Future

LILY DIAMOND

Kale & Caramel: Recipes for Body, Heart, and Table

WAKING UP

GOING OUTSIDE

WITH PEOPLE

IN COMMUNITY

LETTING GO

COMING HOME

TWILIGHT

AT WORK

FACING THE SCREEN

IN YOUR BODY

Of course, you're general, but you're also specific. A citizen and a person. And the person you are is like nobody else on the planet. Nobody has the exact memory that you have. What is now known is not all that you are capable of knowing.

You are your own stories, and therefore free to imagine and experience what it means to be human without wealth. What it feels like to be human without domination over others, without reckless arrogance, without fear of others unlike you, without rotating, rehearsing, and reinventing the hatreds you learned in the sandbox. The theme you choose may change or simply elude you, but being your own story means you can always choose the tone. It also means that you can invent the language to say who you are and what you mean.

But then, I am a teller of stories and therefore an optimist, a believer in the ethical bend of the human heart, a believer in the mind's disgust with fraud and its appetite for truth, a believer in the ferocity of beauty.

So, from my point of view, which is that of a storyteller, I see your life as already artful, waiting, just waiting and ready for you to make it art.

TONI MORRISON

CONTENTS

READY

> **Not everything that
> is faced can be changed.
> But nothing can be
> changed until it is faced.**
>
> JAMES BALDWIN

Do you ever wish you could talk to someone who asked the right questions about every part of your life and being—every single time? Not the easy questions, but the hard ones that draw out your truth. The ones that push you beyond who you are right now, and challenge your ideas about who you can be. These are the sacred questions: the ones that expose how you came to be who you are, and reveal what you must do to become someone else—someone less fearful and more honest, less confused and more, well, free.

Yeah. Us, too. Which is why we spent a decade developing *What's Your Story?*, a process that reveals the old, repetitive stories that shape our lives and transforms the next leg of the journey. This self-inquiry method integrates insights from our combined forty years of personal and political activism, memoir writing, and psychospiritual and psychosomatic practice in Buddhist, Hindu, and Western healing traditions. *What's Your Story?* is for writers, creatives, scientists, psychologists, lawyers, activists, and anyone who longs to bring a new story to life.

In other words, *What's Your Story?* is for you.

You, because you are ready to rewrite the stories of your life that resist all your attempts to change them. The stories that, despite your best efforts, keep you smaller than you want to be. That pattern you keep repeating with romantic partner after romantic partner? You want it to end. The lack of connection you feel in every one of your friendships? You can no longer bear it. The sinking sensation you get in your stomach every time you talk to your family? It's making you sick and you want—no, need—to be well. Those thirty-five minutes you spend in bed each night comparing who you thought you'd be by now to who you actually are? Quite frankly, you'd rather get some sleep. And we'd rather see you well rested.

We wrote this book because we've been where you are or somewhere a lot like it, and we've worked with hundreds of people who have been there, too. Most of us think it's normal to go through life telling the same sad, tired stories about ourselves over and over again until we die.

We don't.

Let's get personal.

When we first met, Lily was grieving her mother's death and a profound heartbreak. In the wake of these losses, a new sense of self emerged from the confines of her day-to-day life as a yoga and philosophy teacher. She recognized a deep internal struggle between the desire to free herself of an identity defined by family, teachers, and friends, and her aching need to belong. She walked into Rebecca's Art of Memoir workshop ready to write an old story, and walked out ready to write a new one. In the process, Lily awakened to her own voice and a fulfilling career inspired by her true passions—as a bestselling author, photographer, and creative agent of change in the food and wellness industries. Through writing and rewriting her story, she released old ideas and welcomed the rich possibilities of an unconditioned mind.

On the other hand, Rebecca had transitioned from a life of feminist activism into a decade-long period of intense Buddhist study. She was living on Maui and balancing a flourishing writing and speaking career with the challenges and delights of raising a curious, energetic, and totally engaging four-year-old. After writing two memoirs and choosing a life that looked very different from her family's expectations, Rebecca was experiencing a profound sense of authenticity, accomplishment, and mastery over her own life and mind. With a heightened awareness of the power of writing to loosen the grip of old stories and make space for the creation of new lives, she convened a seven-day master class, The Art of Memoir, to support people drawn to a more authentic way of living. When Lily walked into the writing room, Rebecca recognized a readiness in her, a quickening that spoke of a shared purpose. And that's when we embarked on a journey that changed both of our stories forever.

Over the next two years, Lily began to assist Rebecca in the workshops. Together we supported participants in excavating and reflecting on the past and exploring new directions for the future. In a community willing to hold the old story while encouraging the birth of the new, something remarkable happened: each person woke up to the awareness that they, too, were entitled to a happy—though not necessarily pain-free or idyllic—ending, and could actually write one for themselves.

Imagining new outcomes and finding freedom from the past seemed not only possible but inevitable. Even as we talked about cancer, child abuse, sexual slavery, the Holocaust, institutionalized racism, parental neglect, poverty, heartbreak, and so much else, we found ourselves fully present and enjoying the process. On the last day of class—exhausted, exhilarated, and transformed—many asked for ongoing tools to embark on a practice of regularly speaking and writing their truth. And for a way to share that practice with others.

From that point of need, What's Your Story? began as a weekly newsletter, and morphed into an in-person course. We developed a series of questions for people who have held themselves and their stories silent for too long. Each question is an access point to healing and growth. Collectively, the questions take the reader through a sequential process of self-inquiry and—if the reader is willing to change—personal transformation.

Those questions became a method, and that method became this book. You are now part of a global community rewriting your story, and in so doing, changing our collective future. While we can't change the hardships we've endured, or ignore the avalanche of forces beyond our control, we can decide what narrative we assign them.

We can, at least in the sanctity of our own minds, write our own stories and reclaim our own power.

The truth is, human beings imagine so often, so thoroughly, and so well that we eventually imagine ourselves. We craft an ever-evolving narrative that shapes our sense of who we are, and who we may become. We make our own meaning. This is what Joan Didion suggests when she says "we tell ourselves stories in order to live."

Ultimately, we believe we all deserve a better story, one that supports a free mind, light spirit, and courageous heart. A story defined by openness and possibility, strength and self-awareness, confidence and the fortitude to stand up for what's right—not just for ourselves but for the world. A story that assures us, in our final hours, that we have lived as the best version of ourselves. We can let go with no regrets.

If you walk down the road of these pages with us, we're going to ask you some hard questions. About you. About your life, your work, your body, your heart, your mind. About the meaning that you've made of it all. We're going to ask you to think, feel, reflect, and listen—more profoundly than ever before—to your answers. Why? So you can change them.

This book is for you, and we are so glad you're here. Whether you choose to share your story with the world or hold this magic notebook as your personal record of self-mastery doesn't matter. It's your gift to yourself, and it's yours to keep however you want. We hope you answer every question, more than once if necessary, and write until you're spent. We even added some blank pages at the back of the book in case you need them.

No matter what, we want you to know you are not alone. We love you. And we will hold your best story for you, even in the moments when you cannot hold it for yourself. We believe in your ability to see yourself to the other side.

So we invite you, right now, to write the story of the next day of your life and the last day of your life—also known as the best story in the whole wide world. Why? Because it's yours. You wrote it, you lived it, you vanquished all comers. You—not your parents or your teachers or your friends or your colleagues or your government—showed up for the party, and guess what? You danced all night.

As yourself.

S
E
T

> We must trust our own thinking.
> Trust where we are going.
> And get the job done.
>
> WILMA MANKILLER

What's Your Story? takes you through the normal sequence of your day: waking up and discovering your body, being in relationship with other people, working, interacting with technology and nature, cultivating community and a home, recovering, reflecting, and reckoning with mortality. In each chapter you will look back, let go, and move forward. You will rigorously assess your thoughts and beliefs, and make decisions to write a more empowering truth into being.

Each chapter will invite you to examine the assumptions and expectations you carry into that particular area of your life. What do we mean by assumptions and expectations? These are ideas you've learned about the way you are, the way other people are, the way the world is and should be. These ideas are passed down from family, parents, and caregivers, they're taken on from friends and colleagues, and they're impressed upon you by any number of sociopolitical, religious, and cultural systems of belief.

For example, for many centuries, scientists maintained that people with different skin colors were genetically distinct, and categorized them into five "races." These assumptions, this *story*, became the foundation of racist ideologies that justify and encourage systemic oppression. Yet when the human genome was mapped in 2000, scientific communities unanimously agreed there is far more genetic variation in people with the *same* skin color than there is between those with different skin colors. In fact, the DNA of all human beings is 99.9 percent the same. This truth tells a far different story about who we are and how we should relate to one another.

Dismantling your assumptions will free you to tell a new story.

WRITING YOUR STORY

Each chapter guides you, step by step, through the vast territory of your mind. In the process, you will acknowledge where you are and how you got there. From a place of stability and safety, begin to imagine a new story for yourself. We will ask you hard questions, but none will be too hard to answer if you really want to know, if you really want to grow, if you really want to write yourself to well-being.

While the book is structured to take you through the cycle of a day, we invite you to write at any time. Perhaps it's stealing a few moments before bed, in your car after dropping the kids at school, or in a bathroom stall at work. Move through *What's Your Story?* in any way that feels most organic to you. Spending a few minutes writing on each inquiry, you could power through each chapter in an hour. Or you could write for two days on a single question.

It's completely up to you.

As you move through your imagined day, you'll notice a number of overlapping themes. If you want to follow one theme at a time, we've woven five thematic tracks through the book; you can follow these tracks by using the color coding on the next page.

For example, if you want to focus on creativity and self-expression, turn to the pages marked with gold. If you need to nurture yourself, seek out questions marked with pink. Feel like rewriting white supremacist heterocapitalism? Focus on the inquiries labeled in cream. And so on.

CREATIVITY AND SELF-EXPRESSION

SELF-CARE

ACTIVISM

SPIRITUALITY

GRIEF, LOSS, AND THE WORK OF HEALING

Finally, a note on best practices: finding the voice to know, write, and perhaps even speak one's story can mean the difference between a life of repressed silence and a life of joyful fulfillment. The bridge between the two can rarely be crossed alone. We recommend finding the support you need to close that gap. This support may come in the form of calling on ancestors; gathering a group of friends to walk through these pages together; or seeking the counsel of a therapist, mentor, or spiritual guide.

And of course we'll be here, too, supporting your every insight.

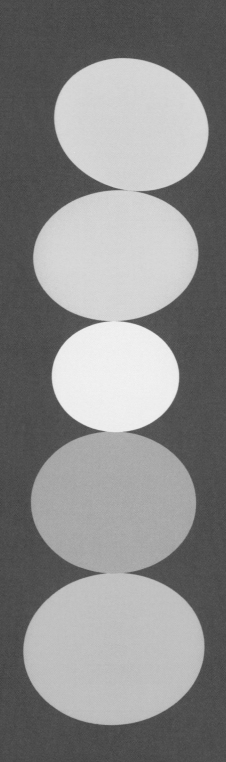

CREATIVITY AND
SELF-EXPRESSION

SELF-CARE

ACTIVISM

SPIRITUALITY

GRIEF, LOSS, AND
THE WORK OF HEALING

G

I am my ancestors' wildest dreams.

BRANDAN ODUMS

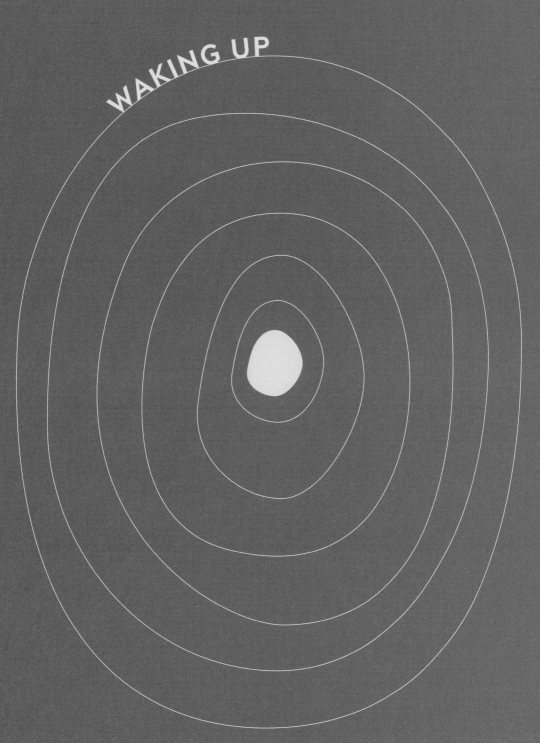

WAKING UP

DO IT

Every story starts somewhere. You, too, began at the beginning, a seed in the dark. And at one singular moment, you opened your eyes to a world of light, sound, and movement.

Every morning you repeat this process, emerging from the quiet of sleep into the noise and chaos of the day. In our first moments of awareness, between sleep and waking, we scramble to pull thoughts, images, and memories from the archives of our life. Piece by piece we assemble a story. Our story.

But waking up doesn't have to happen by rote. And it doesn't just happen in the morning.

Every moment brings the opportunity to awaken and to put ourselves, and our stories, together in a new way. We can reexamine our earliest memories and beliefs about who we are, where we came from, where we are going, and why we are here.

In the split second before we open our eyes, we ask: Who am I? Where am I? What is this bed and this life I am in? How do I make sense of it all?

Use these pages to tell your own story of awakening.

Read each question.

Turn it over in your mind until it
evokes an image, sparks an idea,
or inspires a reflection.

Breathe.

Start writing. Take up all the
space you need.

Write for at least five minutes.

Take another breath.

If there's more to say, keep writing.
Use the blank pages in the back
if you like.

When the words stop coming,
read over what you wrote,
without judgment.

Keep breathing.

Be tender with yourself as you
become aware of your truth and
the emotion it evokes.

Then move on to the next question,
or take a break. Whatever feels
right in the moment.

What is your first memory?
Did you experience it or did someone tell it to you
so many times it came to feel like your own?

How has that memory informed your thoughts about yourself?
How has it shaped your story and your life?

What assumptions do you have about yourself and your life as a result of that memory? Are those expectations serving you? If so, how? If not, how can you commit to changing them?

_____

_____

_____

_____

_____

_____

_____

_____

_____

_____

_____

_____

_____

_____

_____

_____

_____

_____

_____

_____

_____

_____

_____

_____

Who are you, right now? What is the story of your life today?
Who are you when no one is looking?
What do you love and what drives you crazy?

What limits you and what helps you grow?

Make a list of the things that give you total joy, and a
list of the things that make you feel less awesome.

YAY!

1

2

3

4

5

6

7

8

9

10

NAY.

1

2

3

4

5

6

7

8

9

10

What are your assumptions about who, where, and what you should be at this moment in your life?

What do you think it means to be a healthy human
being today, in this world, right now? How are you living up
to those expectations? How are you missing the mark?
How can you get closer to your aspirations?

We all live with a "board of directors": parents, siblings, partners, teachers, spiritual leaders, friends, bosses, and others sit at a big table in our mind, telling us what to do. Use this space to write what each board member says to you.

Now ask them to be quiet, to listen to you, to cooperate.
If they won't, ask them to leave. Fire them if you have to.
In this new silence, ask again, what should you do
with your life? Write down what you hear.

_____

_____

_____

_____

_____

_____

_____

_____

_____

_____

_____

_____

_____

_____

_____

_____

_____

_____

_____

_____

_____

_____

What is your first memory of feeling connected to something greater
than or beyond yourself? How did it make you feel?

How did that memory shape your beliefs about yourself and others?

_____

_____

_____

_____

_____

_____

_____

_____

_____

_____

_____

_____

_____

_____

_____

_____

_____

_____

_____

_____

_____

_____

_____

_____

Why do you think you are here?
What are you supposed to do with the time you have?

Are you living in sync with those beliefs? If not, why not?
What choices can you make today to honor your purpose?

_____

_____

_____

_____

_____

_____

_____

_____

_____

_____

_____

_____

_____

_____

_____

_____

_____

_____

_____

_____

_____

_____

_____

How would you describe your relationship with your mind?

How do you relate to your state of mind over the course of a day?

How can you make your mind an ally?

What are a few of your core beliefs? Do they make you happy?
Do they make the world a better place?

If those beliefs don't make you happy, why do you hold on to them?

_____
_____
_____
_____
_____
_____
_____
_____
_____

Who would you be, and what would the
world look like, if you let them go?

_____
_____
_____
_____
_____
_____
_____
_____
_____
_____
_____
_____

How do you envision your future self? Who and what
is contributing to the creation of this self? How can you play
a more active role in your own becoming?

What concrete steps can you take toward
creating a future self that you love?

_____
_____
_____
_____
_____
_____
_____
_____
_____
_____
_____
_____
_____
_____
_____
_____
_____
_____
_____
_____
_____
_____
_____
_____
_____

Agency starts with our awareness of our subtle sensory, body-based feelings: the greater that awareness, the greater our potential to control our lives. Knowing what we feel is the first step to knowing why we feel that way. If we are aware of the constant changes in our inner and outer environment, we can mobilize to manage them.

BESSEL VAN DER KOLK

DO IT

IN YOUR BODY

We wake up. We roll over. We are bombarded with the realities of living in a body. The body needs to pee. It wants to have sex, or it absolutely does not. It smells bad, or strange, or mysterious—oh no, an infection? A rash? An ache in the joints? It encounters other bodies. It houses our mind, our hopes, our anxieties, our heart.

Our body demands food, nourishment, attention, strength, time. It rarely behaves as we wish it would. And every day, it betrays us as it marches, inexorably, toward death. Somehow, though, we must reckon with our body. Through it we tell our story.

Waking up in our body, we ask: How does my body feel? What should I feed it? Is it clean? Where is it required to go? What is my body saying to me? How do I have to present my body to navigate the various spaces I must occupy in the world?

And then, of course, we must be in our body with other bodies. We spend hours, maybe even years, telling ourselves stories about what others think of our body. And we, too, tell stories of theirs: How do I relate to other bodies? How do I share my body? How do I claim my desire? Do I feel safe as a sexual being?

How do I make peace with my body, and learn to heed its subtle—or not so subtle—messages?

Our bodies have their own stories to tell. Use the pages that follow to let yours speak.

Read each question.

Turn it over in your mind until it
evokes an image, sparks an idea,
or inspires a reflection.

Breathe.

Start writing. Take up all the
space you need.

Write for at least five minutes.

Take another breath.

If there's more to say, keep writing.
Use the blank pages in the back
if you like.

When the words stop coming,
read over what you wrote,
without judgment.

Keep breathing.

Be tender with yourself as you
become aware of your truth and the
way it feels in your cells, muscles,
and bones.

Then move on to the next question,
or take a break. Whatever feels
right in the moment.

What are the first thoughts you remember having about your body? Did those thoughts come from you, your family, a partner, or the media and culture around you?

Which of those messages do you still carry, and which can be let go?

_____
_____
_____
_____
_____
_____
_____
_____
_____
_____
_____
_____
_____
_____
_____
_____
_____
_____
_____
_____
_____
_____
_____
_____
_____

What are your expectations for your body?
How should it look and feel? What should it be able to do?

How do those expectations support or hinder your well-being?

_____

_____

_____

_____

_____

_____

_____

_____

_____

_____

_____

_____

_____

_____

_____

_____

_____

_____

_____

_____

_____

_____

_____

_____

_____

_____

How do you nourish your body? How can you be more honest
with yourself about the food you eat, where it comes from,
and how it makes you feel?

What specific changes can you make to bring a greater
sense of ease to your relationship with food?

_____

_____

_____

_____

_____

_____

_____

_____

_____

_____

_____

_____

_____

_____

_____

_____

_____

_____

_____

_____

_____

_____

_____

_____

_____

How would you describe your body? Flexible, strong, stiff, weak, supple, resistant? How do you feel moving in your body now—and how would you like to feel?

What can you do to create a sense of physical equanimity and freedom?

Make a list of all the positions, places, and situations
that make your body feel alive and excited. Make a list of all
the positions, places, and situations that do not.

YAY!

NAY.

1

1

2

2

3

3

4

4

5

5

6

6

7

7

8

8

9

9

10

10

In what ways do you feel your body betrays you or has betrayed you in the past? In what ways have you betrayed your body?

What can you do to address those betrayals and
restore trust and wholeness in your body?

_____
_____
_____
_____
_____
_____
_____
_____
_____
_____
_____
_____
_____
_____
_____
_____
_____
_____
_____
_____
_____
_____
_____
_____
_____

What is your first memory of sexual pleasure?
What did that experience awaken in you, and how is that
awareness still present with you today?

What turns you on?

_____
_____
_____
_____
_____
_____
_____
_____
_____
_____
_____
_____

Do you make time to cultivate sexual pleasure? Why? Why not?

_____
_____
_____
_____
_____
_____
_____
_____
_____
_____
_____
_____
_____
_____

IN YOUR BODY

What is sex like for you, with a partner (or partners) or on your own?

After sex, I feel:

alive	silly	bored
shy	famous	exhausted
energetic	aggressive	eager
better	thankful	clumsy
vulnerable	gifted	emotional
fine	agreeable	devoted
recharged	victorious	defeated
generous	sacred	uncomfortable
diminished	ambitious	gentle
creative	witty	electric
uninterested	helpful	exploited
polite	brave	happy
dead	wonderful	sleepy
vast	important	powerful
proud	calm	sexy
mellow	juicy	hungry
wrong	delightful	abundant

_____ _____ _____

_____ _____ _____

_____ _____ _____

How would you see, speak to, and touch your body if it belonged to the person you loved most in the world?

Start a loving dialogue with your body. Write it here.

Relationships are stories.

ESTHER PEREL

WITH PEOPLE

DO IT

We wake, we breathe, we relate. From the very beginning, we are profoundly interconnected with the people who conceive, nurture, and sustain us. As we grow up, our web of relationship expands, and our experiences of togetherness become more complex. That matrix of connection—and each human within it—shapes our sense of where we begin and end, and the stories we tell about who we are.

Most importantly, we absorb a story *about* relationship, about how we should relate to others and how they should relate to us. This narrative emerges from our families, teachers, friends, and the larger political narratives of the world in which we live. It shapes every encounter, conversation, and act of intimacy.

Being with people, we ask: How close do I want to be to another person? What do they bring to my development as a human being? Who do I allow in my life, and who do I keep out? Which behaviors, words, and actions make me feel valued, and how do I ask for them? How do I show up for others? What is the role of human connection in my life?

We have no stories without relationship, and no relationships without stories. Use these pages to tell yours.

Read each question.

Turn it over in your mind until it
evokes an image, sparks an idea,
or inspires a reflection.

Breathe.

Start writing. Take up all the
space you need.

Write for at least five minutes.

Take another breath.

If there's more to say, keep writing.
Use the blank pages in the back
if you like.

When the words stop coming,
read over what you wrote,
without judgment.

Keep breathing.

Be tender with yourself as you
become aware of your truth
and what it reveals about your
relationships.

Then move on to the next question,
or take a break. Whatever feels
right in the moment.

What are your assumptions about people, as a whole? Are they well-intentioned, loving, kind, cruel, selfish, compassionate?

How do these thoughts shape your behavior
in all of the relationships in your life?

What do you expect from your friends, family members, partner(s), and children, if you have them? How are you treated by the people you love?

How do you want to be treated by the people you love?

Conversely, what do you think is expected of you?
How do you want to treat the people you love?

_____
_____
_____
_____
_____
_____
_____
_____
_____
_____
_____
_____
_____
_____
_____
_____
_____
_____
_____
_____
_____
_____
_____
_____
_____
_____

WITH PEOPLE

What do people in your family think of you? What is the story of you within your family? How has that story informed your behaviors and relationships with friends, teachers, and romantic partners?

If you could be the sole author of that story, what would you write?

_____

_____

_____

_____

_____

_____

_____

_____

_____

_____

_____

_____

_____

_____

_____

_____

_____

_____

_____

_____

_____

_____

_____

_____

_____

_____

Who have you lost—friends, family, lovers, partners—and how did those losses change you and the story of your life?

Where are you in the process of healing from those losses?
What have you discovered about yourself from the healing process?

_____

_____

_____

_____

_____

_____

_____

_____

_____

_____

_____

_____

_____

_____

_____

_____

_____

_____

_____

_____

_____

_____

_____

_____

How do the people you allow into your most
private spaces make you feel? Vulnerable or courageous?
Shameful or prideful? Burdened or uplifted?

What types of people, relationships, and intimate
behaviors are you habitually drawn to? What do you get from
returning to those people, relationships, and behaviors?

Who in your life gives you as much as you give them? Who makes you laugh and feel good about yourself? Who makes you feel connected, alive, and supported in the world? Write a little about each person and what they do that makes you feel good.

I feel loved when   does

I feel valued when   does

I feel known when   does

I feel safe when   does

How easy is it for you to express and receive love?
If one is easier than the other, which one and why?

How do you communicate?
Are you better at listening or speaking? Why?

What would you need to change in order
to be a more skillful communicator?

_____

_____

_____

_____

_____

_____

_____

_____

_____

_____

_____

_____

_____

_____

_____

_____

_____

_____

_____

_____

_____

How do you cultivate healthy intimacy with others?
Are you able to establish appropriate boundaries? If yes, how?
If no, why not? What stories do your boundaries tell?

How can you become more skillful at caring
for yourself within relationships?

_____
_____
_____
_____
_____
_____
_____
_____
_____
_____
_____
_____
_____
_____
_____
_____
_____
_____
_____
_____
_____
_____

WITH PEOPLE

What kinds of relationships are most important to you? Family, friends, professional colleagues, romantic partners?

In an ideal world, how much time and energy would you spend on each of those categories? Make a pie chart, dividing your time and energy in a visible way. Color code it. What story does this chart tell? How does it sync with or deviate from your overall view of a happy life?

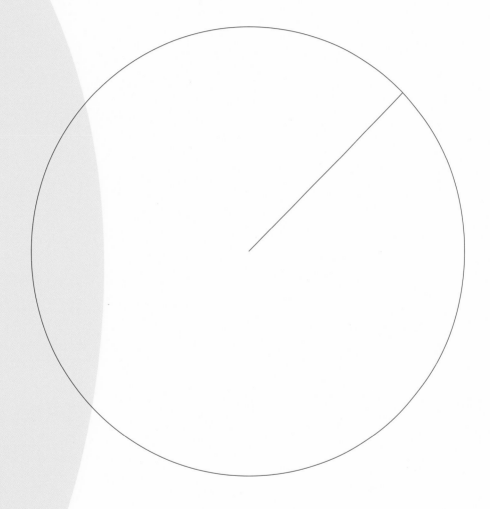

My job, I realized, was to be myself,
to speak as myself. And so I did.

MICHELLE OBAMA

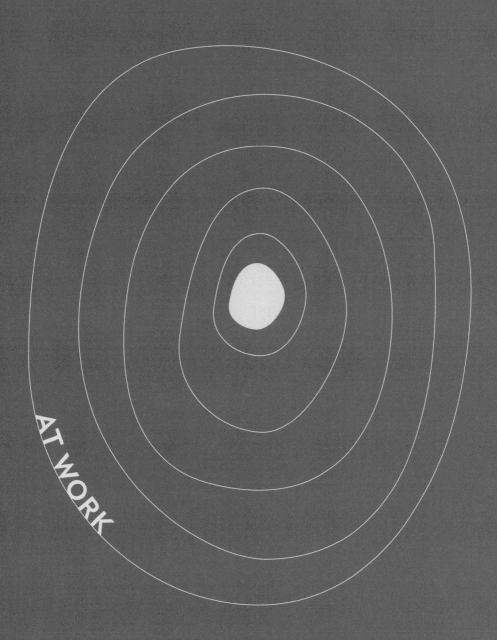

DO IT

AT WORK

As children, we're encouraged to mine the depths of our imaginations when asked what we want to be when we grow up. An astronaut! A neurosurgeon! The first female Mexican American Buddhist president of the United States! The sky is the limit. Until we grow up, and the narrative shifts. "Be realistic!" we're told. There's rent to pay, after all, and bills that never end.

At some point, thinking about work goes from dreaming about the future to battling to survive.

Whether we like it or not, hypercapitalism is a dominant, determining system in our lives. Whether you work eighty-hour weeks at three different jobs or do the labor of (at least) five humans as a full-time parent, the stories of the work you do inevitably define your time here on earth.

At work, we ask: What do I feel called to do? What is work to me? How do I feel about working on a team or working on my own? How do I relate to money? How am I using the currency of my own energy in the world?

Is my work an expression of what I care about and who I want to be?

Read each question.

Turn it over in your mind until it
evokes an image, sparks an idea,
or inspires a reflection.

Breathe.

Start writing. Take up all the
space you need.

Write for at least five minutes.

Take another breath.

If there's more to say, keep writing.
Use the blank pages in the back
if you like.

When the words stop coming,
read over what you wrote,
without judgment.

Keep breathing.

Be tender with yourself as you
become aware of your truth and
what it means for your future.

Then move on to the next question,
or take a break. Whatever feels
right in the moment.

What did you want to be when you grew up? Why?

Did you follow that dream? Why? Why not?

What are your beliefs about work? How much time should you spend working? How much money should you make?

Do you seek fulfillment from your work, or are you comfortable with a simple exchange of your energy for money? Does this way of thinking about work make you happy? Why or why not?

Where do you think money comes from? Who has the most money, and why? Who doesn't, and why?

What should you do with the money you have? What shouldn't you do?
Where did you get these ideas? How are they serving you?

Where does your money come from now, and where
would you like it to come from in the future?

How much money do you really need?

Do you think you deserve to be financially comfortable?
Why? Why not?

Do you see yourself as someone who can set a goal and achieve it? Why or why not?

When was the first time you were able to accomplish a goal,
however big or small? How did it make you feel?

_____

_____

_____

_____

_____

_____

_____

_____

_____

_____

_____

Did you build on that experience going forward? Why? Why not?

_____

_____

_____

_____

_____

_____

_____

_____

_____

_____

_____

_____

_____

Make a list of the major players involved in your work. If you work with others, you might consider your coworkers, managers, or supervisors. If you're self-employed, consider your clients, colleagues, collaborators, and online communities.

Who do you enjoy working with, and why?
How can you cultivate more partnerships of that kind?

What activities make you feel accomplished,
masterful, and most authentically yourself?

How often do you do these activities, and with whom?

Which parts of yourself come out to play when you do these things?
How can you integrate more play into your daily life?

_____

_____

_____

_____

_____

_____

_____

_____

_____

_____

_____

_____

_____

_____

_____

_____

_____

_____

_____

_____

_____

_____

_____

_____

Does your work fuel your creativity?
Is that important to you? Why or why not?

I am most creative when:

_____

_____

_____

_____

_____

_____

_____

_____

_____

_____

_____

_____

_____

_____

_____

_____

_____

_____

_____

_____

_____

_____

_____

_____

_____

_____

_____

AT WORK

Do you take risks in your work and your daily life?
If yes, why? If no, why not?

What are you willing to risk to feel a sense of fulfillment?

If you could successfully do anything you wanted from start to finish, if you could take an unprecedented risk and know that you'd be entirely supported, what would you do?

How would completing that venture make you feel?
How might it change the way you see yourself?

_____

_____

_____

_____

_____

_____

_____

_____

_____

_____

_____

_____

_____

_____

_____

_____

_____

_____

_____

_____

_____

_____

_____

_____

_____

AT WORK

It's seductive
to assume that data
is knowledge.

TONI MORRISON

Information will never
replace illumination.

SUSAN SONTAG

DO IT

FACING THE SCREEN

Be honest: What's the first thing you reach for when you wake up in the morning? For many, it's not the warm body of a partner or pet, but a cool, hard piece of glass and metal. Since the advent of the internet (and more recently, those hand extensions known as smartphones), research has shown that we've become less in control of our time and attention. Today, the average person spends up to eleven hours a day looking at a screen. Much of that time is spent on social media platforms that replicate the addictive mechanisms of casinos, increasing levels of anxiety and depression.

These days, we get almost everything from our technology. Illuminated screens deliver a constant flow of algorithmically dictated content to our fingertips, allowing us to procure everything from a ride to work to a carton of breast milk. Even as we participate in so-called digital togetherness, the plunging self-esteem of social media users tells another story. So do the clinical studies on the dangers of electromagnetic radiation and the blue light emanating from our screens.

Facing our screens, we ask: If time is my most precious resource, how do I manage the relentless seduction of technology? In the midst of constant digital distraction, how do I sustain a state of contemplation, long considered necessary for creativity and complex problem solving?

Delve into these questions as obsessively as you would your next Netflix binge.

Read each question.

Turn it over in your mind until it
evokes an image, sparks an idea,
or inspires a reflection.

Breathe.

Start writing. Take up all the
space you need.

Write for at least five minutes.

Take another breath.

If there's more to say, keep writing.
Use the blank pages in the back
if you like.

When the words stop coming,
read over what you wrote,
without judgment.

Resist the urge to check out of your
process and into your technology.

Be tender with yourself as you
become aware of the truth of your
relationship with technology and
what it says about your life.

Then move on to the next question,
or take a break. Whatever feels
right in the moment.

What are your assumptions about technology? Do you think it brings progress or devolution, enlightenment or confusion? Why?

Do you feel in alignment or at odds with the ways you use technology in your life? How so? What is the cost (monetary, mental, emotional) of using technology in these ways?

_____

_____

_____

_____

_____

_____

_____

_____

_____

_____

_____

_____

_____

_____

_____

_____

_____

_____

_____

_____

_____

_____

_____

How do you use technology throughout the day? To track your sleep? Communicate with your family? Run your business? Find love? Work out? List all the ways you use technology to shape and support your life.

Can you remember a time in your life when
technology was not ever-present? Where were you,
who were you with, and how did you spend your time?

_____

_____

_____

_____

_____

_____

_____

_____

_____

_____

_____

_____

_____

_____

_____

_____

_____

_____

_____

_____

_____

_____

_____

_____

_____

Who are you when you are facing a screen, and who are you when you are not? Do you feel a difference in your body and mind in each space?

Note the sensations.
Return to this page and add to the list as you notice new things.

SCREEN

_____

_____

_____

_____

_____

_____

_____

_____

_____

_____

_____

_____

_____

_____

_____

_____

_____

_____

_____

_____

_____

_____

NO SCREEN

_____

_____

_____

_____

_____

_____

_____

_____

_____

_____

_____

_____

_____

_____

_____

_____

_____

_____

_____

_____

FACING THE SCREEN

What is your approach to the life that you live on social media?
Who are you on social media and who do others seem to be?

What decisions have gone into crafting your online persona?
What values do those decisions reflect?

_____
_____
_____
_____
_____
_____
_____
_____
_____
_____
_____
_____
_____
_____
_____
_____
_____
_____
_____
_____
_____
_____
_____
_____
_____

How do technology and social media affect your relationships?
Do you enjoy spending time with people in real life, or are you more
comfortable dealing with them through screens?

What story do these preferences tell about your
future and the future of our human family?

_____

_____

_____

_____

_____

_____

_____

_____

_____

_____

_____

_____

_____

_____

_____

_____

_____

_____

_____

_____

_____

_____

_____

_____

_____

_____

_____

_____

What does privacy mean to you in a world where almost anything can be found out by anyone online? How do you maintain or relinquish control of your privacy?

What is most important to keep private, for yourself and others?

Do you believe you are addicted to technology?
Have you ever tried to change your relationship to technology?
What did you do? What happened when you tried to change?

Describe one tech habit you do on a regular basis by rote.
Describe how you're going to break the habit.

Every day I

on my device because

Tomorrow I am going to

on my device because

Share this with a friend and ask for their
support or invite them to join you.

Think about how you want to use technology:
for social change, relationship building, creative expression,
or another application we have yet to imagine?
What habits can you cultivate to honor this vision?

On the next page, write a mission statement that
reflects your intentions. Place it above your computer
or anywhere else you will see it frequently.

TECHNOLOGY + ME

I want to use technology for:

I am going to do that by:

We can't meaningfully proceed with healing, with restoration, without "re-story-ation." In other words, our relationship with the land cannot heal until we hear its stories. But who will tell them?

ROBIN WALL KIMMERER

GOING OUTSIDE

DO IT

No matter how many walls or screens we surround ourselves with, we must inevitably come face-to-face with the world outside. Light, water, blades of grass tickling the bottoms of our feet, a coyote howling in the canyon, a stalwart dandelion forcing its way through city sidewalks. Nature is there—providing for us, holding us, speaking to us, waiting for us.

Imagining ourselves as separate from—and having dominion over—nature, we forget that we, too, are animals. We forget that we live on land rich with history, pain, and beauty, deeply burdened by the weight of our presence. We forget that each of us is responsible for the legacy and survival of the earth.

Going outside, we ask: Where do I live? How do I relate to the air, the dirt, the trees, the stars? Do I notice the earth around me, in city or country? Do I see the environment as something separate from me? Who lived on this land before me? Do I contribute to the health of the planet? Do I understand there is no "away"—that this earth is the only home we have?

Stories about the earth are told to us every day. What stories do you wish were being told?

Use these pages as fertile soil from which new narratives of the earth might grow. What story will you tell?

Read each question.

Turn it over in your mind until it
evokes an image, sparks an idea,
or inspires a reflection.

Breathe.

Start writing. Take up all the
space you need.

Write for at least five minutes.

Take another breath.

If there's more to say, keep writing.
Use the blank pages in the back
if you like.

When the words stop coming,
read over what you wrote,
without judgment.

Keep breathing. Let each breath be
a conduit to bring the outside in.

Be tender with yourself as you
become aware of your truth and
what it means to be one small part
of an interdependent universe.

Then move on to the next question,
or take a break. Whatever feels
right in the moment.

What is your first memory of being outside in nature?
What smells, colors, textures, sounds, and tastes do you remember?

How did being outside make you feel then?
And how does it make you feel now?

_____

_____

_____

_____

_____

_____

_____

_____

_____

_____

_____

_____

_____

_____

_____

_____

_____

_____

_____

_____

_____

GOING OUTSIDE

What story did your family tell you about nature, and what
your relationship to nature should look like? Did that
story make you feel more or less comfortable in nature?
More connected to or separate from the earth?

Is your nature story the same now, or different? How?

_____
_____
_____
_____
_____
_____
_____
_____
_____
_____
_____
_____
_____
_____
_____
_____
_____
_____
_____
_____
_____
_____
_____
_____
_____
_____

The places where you grew up left imprints on your mind and
body, teaching you what to trust, what to fear, how to move.
What lands, cities, or suburbs shaped you?

How have those experiences shaped the way
you relate to outdoor environments?

Make a list of the places where you feel safe, and
another of the places where you feel unsafe.

SAFE

_____

_____

_____

_____

_____

_____

_____

_____

UNSAFE

_____

_____

_____

_____

_____

_____

_____

_____

What steps can you take to stay balanced and
sane wherever you may find yourself?

_____

_____

_____

_____

_____

_____

_____

_____

_____

_____

_____

What do you expect the earth to provide? In what ways
do you believe it should sustain you? Should it provide you with
clean air and water, and give you shelter? Do you expect
its resources to be unlimited? Why or why not?

Consider what it costs the earth to provide you with those things. How does that make you feel?

_____
_____
_____
_____
_____
_____
_____
_____
_____
_____
_____
_____
_____
_____
_____
_____
_____
_____
_____
_____
_____
_____
_____

Do you drive a car, or use other forms of transport? What kind of food do you eat? What products do you buy and use on your body? How much waste do you produce, and what do you do with it? Are there better choices you might make for yourself and the earth?

How do your feelings about the environment and our changing climate inform the choices you make every day?

Make a list of ten things you could
do differently for the planet.

1 _____

2 _____

3 _____

4 _____

5 _____

6 _____

7 _____

8 _____

9 _____

10 _____

Who lived before you—centuries and millennia ago—on the land where you live now? If you don't know, do a simple online search to learn the answer.

The people who lived here 1,000 years ago called themselves

They believed

about the natural world.

The people who live here now call themselves

They believe

about the natural world.

How does it make you feel to uncover this history, to sit with its implications in your own life and the story of our collective culture? How can it inform the choices you make in your life today?

_____
_____
_____
_____
_____
_____
_____
_____
_____
_____
_____
_____
_____
_____
_____
_____
_____
_____
_____
_____
_____
_____
_____
_____
_____

Billions of people live and depend on the earth—what, if any, are our responsibilities to each other?

What kinds of conversations should we be having with people
in other countries—as one human community—about these issues?
How might you engage in these conversations?

_____

_____

_____

_____

_____

_____

_____

_____

_____

_____

_____

_____

_____

_____

_____

_____

_____

_____

_____

_____

_____

_____

Who are you when you allow yourself to revel in nature,
to be fully immersed and full of appreciation?

How does it feel to consider yourself a part of,
rather than separate from, the natural world? What keeps
you from feeling this every day?

What changes do you expect to see on earth in your lifetime? If our planet becomes uninhabitable, for instance, what will you do? What actions will you wish you had taken? How would you feel if you or future generations had to move to another planet to survive?

Write a new story of your relationship with the earth.

If you have come here to help me,
you are wasting your time. But if you
have come because your liberation is
bound up with mine, then let us
work together.

LILLA WATSON

A dream you dream alone
is only a dream. A dream you
dream together is reality.

YOKO ONO

IN COMMUNITY

DO IT

Imagine yourself as the focal point, the absolute center of a number of concentric, sometimes overlapping circles. The closest, smallest circle is your immediate family. The next, your neighbors and your neighborhood. Then your friends and extended family, and so on, until you reach the outer limits of your town, your state, your country, the planet, even the interstellar space we share with galaxies beyond.

This is your community, and it is exactly this broad—and this specific.

Community demands that we consider who we are in relationship to each of these spheres of existence and what our responsibility is to the beings (human, animal, plant, and otherwise) that live within them. But community is also a feeling, a sense of belonging, a way of being that unites people in common cause. It is the beginning of an impulse to action—to do good for the betterment of those we love and those we do not yet know. It is embodied in principles such as the seventh-generation stewardship of the Iroquois Confederacy, and practices such as intersectional activism and solidarity.

Community acknowledges that no single one of us can be happy and free until all of us are happy and free.

Being in community, we ask: What is my community, and who am I within it? What do I take from and give back to my community? How is my community a reflection of the larger state and country I live in? How do I connect with, listen to, and support people and ideas from outside my immediate community? What do I stand for? And is my understanding of the interdependence of all people and things reflected in the way I live my life?

More than ever before, we now see the importance of people sharing their stories, and how truth-telling changes not just the tellers but also the listeners, and thus the world.

Write your stories of community in these pages. Write a new world.

Read each question.

Turn it over in your mind until it
evokes an image, sparks an idea,
or inspires a reflection.

Breathe.

Start writing. Take up all the
space you need.

Write for at least five minutes.

Take another breath.

If there's more to say, keep writing.
Use the blank pages in the back
if you like.

When the words stop coming,
read over what you wrote,
without judgment.

Keep breathing.

Be tender with yourself as you
become aware of your truth and
what it means about who you are in
community.

Then move on to the next question,
share a question with someone in
your community, or take a break.

Whatever feels right in the moment.

What is your first memory of being part of a community?
What conversations did you hear, what ideas were exchanged,
what rituals did you see? How did people look, move, and
speak differently than—or the same as—you?

Did you feel you belonged? Why or why not?

What did this teach you about belonging? What did it teach you about being an active participant in a community?

_____
_____
_____
_____
_____
_____
_____
_____
_____
_____
_____
_____
_____
_____
_____
_____
_____
_____
_____
_____
_____
_____
_____
_____

What community or communities do you consider yourself a part of? What parts of yourself do you bring to each? What parts do you leave behind?

List these communities, how you are different within each, and how this makes you feel. How does this code-switching serve you? How does it not?

What are your assumptions about what each of your communities should do for you, and what you should do for them?

What should other communities—geographic, religious, cultural—do for you, and what should you do for them?

Whose stories are uplifted and spoken in your communities,
and whose are diminished or silenced?

Where does your story place you within each community?
At the center? At the margin?

How does this place shape the story you tell about your
relationship with that community? How does it make you feel
about being a part of that community?

_____

_____

_____

_____

_____

_____

_____

_____

_____

_____

_____

_____

_____

_____

_____

_____

_____

_____

_____

_____

_____

_____

_____

_____

Which people, places, and ideas in your various communities do you really care about? Who and what do you leave behind?

What do you feel apathetic about that you notice
other people investing in deeply? Why?
How does this serve you?

Make a list of the agreements you have made—consciously or unconsciously—with the people and communities in your life. An agreement might be keeping your word, spending your money on certain objects or donating to specific organizations, eating or acting in ways that reflect your values, or giving your time and energy.

Which of these agreements give you a feeling of
integrity, authenticity, and direction?

_____
_____
_____
_____
_____
_____
_____
_____
_____
_____
_____

How can you continue to honor these moving forward?

_____
_____
_____
_____
_____
_____
_____
_____
_____
_____
_____
_____
_____
_____

Which people, places, and traditions have your communities lost?

How do these losses intersect with your own?
Write that story.

_____

_____

_____

_____

_____

_____

_____

_____

_____

_____

_____

_____

_____

_____

_____

_____

_____

_____

_____

_____

_____

_____

_____

_____

_____

Who do you stand with now? How will you cultivate
a greater sense of belonging, within yourself
and with others?

Celebrate your current story of community, or write a new one.

_____

_____

_____

_____

_____

_____

_____

_____

_____

_____

_____

_____

_____

_____

_____

_____

_____

_____

_____

_____

_____

_____

IN COMMUNITY

Maybe a house is a machine to slow
down time, a barrier against history, a
hope that nothing will happen, though
something always does.

REBECCA SOLNIT

African-American people believed
that the construction of a homeplace,
however fragile and tenuous . . . had a
radical dimension . . . One's homeplace
was the one site where one could freely
construct the issue of humanization,
where one could resist.

bell hooks

You only are free when you realize
you belong no place—you belong
every place—no place at all.

MAYA ANGELOU

DO IT

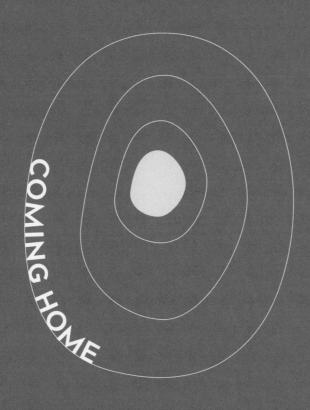

COMING HOME

After the slog of each day—the errands, the work, the doctor's appointments, the constant reckoning with self, community, and nature (microaggressions and climate change, anyone?)—we come home. Home, to whatever patch of land or floor, apartment or room we hope will give us shelter and rest, and allow us to be our most naked and comfortable selves.

As children we are presented with a set of circumstances that we call home. As grown-ups, home takes on a different meaning—a place we must find, make anew, or boldly claim for ourselves. Home is never guaranteed.

Coming home, we ask: What is home to me? What textures, colors, sounds, smells, and tastes soothe me? Where am I able to rest? How do I create a space that is a shelter from the chaos of life? Who represents home to me? What homes have I lost, and have I truly released them? Is home an experience—a state of being—that is beyond the built environment?

Use these pages to write your own homecoming. To revisit the homeplaces of childhood and imagine the sacred spaces of your future.

Read each question.

Turn it over in your mind until it
evokes an image, sparks an idea,
or inspires a reflection.

Breathe.

Start writing. Take up all the
space you need.

Write for at least five minutes.

Take another breath.

If there's more to say, keep writing.
Use the blank pages in the back
if you like.

When the words stop coming,
read over what you wrote,
without judgment.

Keep breathing.

Be tender with yourself as you
become aware of your truth and
what home means to you.

Then move on to the next question,
or take a break. Whatever feels
right in the moment.

What are your first memories of home?
Pick one of those memories and tell its story.

What are the smells, sounds, tastes, textures, or objects that
created your sense of home?

_____

_____

_____

_____

_____

_____

_____

_____

_____

_____

_____

_____

_____

_____

_____

_____

_____

_____

_____

_____

_____

_____

_____

How has your sense of home changed as you have grown from a child to a teenager, from a young adult to a grown-up? What about as you have changed roles, from striving to established (or the reverse), from single person to partner or parent?

Describe your home today, and how it makes you feel.

_____

_____

_____

_____

_____

_____

_____

_____

_____

_____

_____

_____

_____

_____

_____

_____

_____

_____

_____

_____

_____

_____

_____

_____

_____

What homes have you lost, and have you released them?
Tell the story of a few of those homes and who you were in them.

What elements do you want to carry forward from each of these
places and what elements do you want to leave behind?

Make a list of meaningful homes you've lived in and one thing
they gave you—a window seat for reading, a room large enough
for a bed for you and a lover, your independence. Then name
one thing each place took away: an intact family, privacy to
explore your body, silence to think deeply. Thank each home,
and let it go to make space for new homes to come.

PLACE	GAVE	TOOK

What are your visions and dreams of home? How do you want it to look and feel? Who do you want to live there? How do you want people to relate to one another in your home?

What should home provide that can't be found anywhere else?

How does the place where you live now make you feel?
Safe, nurtured, taken care of? What feelings does it
evoke? Sadness, instability, fear? Inner strength,
self-confidence, peace of mind?

Do you call this place home? Why or why not?

What do you need to create a home—a space
where you can thrive, grow, and become?

What do you need to prioritize right now to meet those needs?

Consider whether it is possible for home to be something other than an actual physical space. How might home be a state of mind, a way of being that you carry with you no matter where you go?

How might your body—something that cannot be taken away—be your home, allowing you to move freely, with more confidence and a sense of greater control and self-sufficiency? What is the story there? Try it on.

Now that you know what home means to you,
write a new story of homecoming.

Use this space to draw, sketch, doodle, imagine
what your homeplace might look like.

The best thing about time passing is the privilege of running out of it, of watching the wave of mortality break over me and everyone I know. No more time, no more potential. The privilege of ruling things out. Finishing. Knowing I'm finished. And knowing time will go on without me.

Look at me, dancing my little dance for a few moments against the background of eternity.

SARAH MANGUSO

DO IT

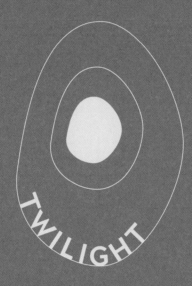

TWILIGHT

There is a stillness at dusk that calls to us from the in-between, a tender space from which new reflections, insights, and actions might arise. As evening comes each day, and in the cycle of our lives, we prepare our bodies and minds for rest, renewal, and ultimately, completion. This is the time to make sense of the stories we have lived and our participation in writing them.

In twilight we come to terms with the finite nature of our lives: our efforts here on earth are limited. Our mortality, the reality of death that shadows us from our first breath, now comes into view. We realize our story is coming to a close, and understand that we alone are responsible for writing its final chapters.

We ask: What did I expect to happen—today, and in my life? What actually happened? How did my choices impact my story? What have I lost? What have I gained? Am I able to rest deeply, in my body and mind? What is the end of my story, and does it reflect my aspirations?

Coming to terms with our mortality is a story in and of itself. Use these pages to face it without fear.

Read each question.

Turn it over in your mind until it
evokes an image, sparks an idea,
or inspires a reflection.

Breathe.

Start writing. Take up all the
space you need.

Write for at least five minutes.

Take another breath.

If there's more to say, keep writing.
Use the blank pages in the back
if you like.

When the words stop coming,
read over what you wrote,
without judgment.

Keep breathing.

Be tender with yourself as you
become aware of your truth and
what it means to live comfortably
with your mortality.

Then move on to the next question,
or take a break. Whatever feels
right in the moment.

What are your thoughts about death and dying?
As you contemplate your mortality, what do you
feel in your body, heart, and mind?

Do you welcome death or turn away from it? Why?

_____

_____

_____

_____

_____

_____

_____

_____

_____

_____

_____

_____

_____

_____

_____

_____

_____

_____

_____

_____

_____

_____

_____

_____

What is your first memory of death?
Who was there, what did you see, what did you hear?
How did you feel?

What did you decide about death in that moment?

_____
_____
_____
_____
_____
_____
_____
_____
_____
_____
_____
_____
_____
_____
_____
_____
_____
_____
_____
_____
_____
_____
_____
_____

How do you define a life well lived?

What is most important to you?

When everything else is gone, I have faith in:

I will cultivate that by:

_____
_____
_____
_____
_____
_____
_____
_____
_____
_____
_____
_____
_____
_____
_____
_____
_____
_____
_____
_____
_____
_____
_____
_____
_____
_____
_____

TWILIGHT

Aside from a peaceful physical transition, what do you think makes a good death? Have you been who you need to be to truly let go, to be at peace? Why? Why not?

In order to die a good death, I need to

I'm having trouble doing this because

If I don't do this, I will die feeling

When you die, what legacy do you want
to leave behind, and to whom?

What do you believe comes after death—an adventure, a reunion with loved ones in a holy place, the liberation of your consciousness from your physical body, nothing at all?

Are you ready to travel into this great unknown?
How can you get ready? Write the story of preparing
for the biggest journey of your life.

There is only one important point you must keep in your mind, and let it be your guide. No matter what people call you, you are just who you are. Keep to this truth. You must ask yourself how is it you want to live your life. We live and we die; this is the truth that we can only face alone. No one can help us, not even the Buddha. So consider carefully, what prevents you from living the way you want to live your life?

HIS HOLINESS THE 14TH DALAI LAMA

LETTING GO

DO IT

What now?

You've written and rewritten the most urgent and intimate stories of your life. And, paying close attention, you've arrived at this knowing: stories are malleable narratives we weave and unravel, weave and unravel, defining ourselves again and again. Each version we write, each story we tell, has the power to limit or liberate us.

But in the end, true freedom lies in letting go of our stories. In relinquishing our fixed narratives about self and world. In liberating ourselves from the story of who we were, who we are, and who we will be. In remembering that we exist beyond words, concepts, and ideas of this world and the next.

This letting go is perhaps our best story of all.

Remember:

Every day is an awakening.
Every day is a new story.
Every day is the beginning,
the middle,
and the end.

Use these final pages to get to the heart of your own freedom.

These pages, and this book, are now your personal touchstone of self-inquiry, deep reflection, and limitless possibility.

Thank you for showing up, doing the work, and having the courage to write your own story. We can't wait to hear it.

Love,

Rebecca & Lily

LILY DIAMOND is a writer, photographer, and advocate harnessing the power of digital media to democratize wellness and empower women through storytelling, accessible practices for inner and outer nourishment, and revolutionary acts of self-care within our earth and human communities. She is the creator of internationally beloved blog Kale & Caramel and author of bestselling memoir-cookbook *Kale & Caramel: Recipes for Body, Heart, and Table*, celebrated as one of the top cookbooks of 2017 by the *New York Times*, *The Independent*, *Cooking Light*, mindbodygreen, and more.

Lily's writing has appeared in *VICE*, Healthyish, the *Huffington Post*, *Better Homes & Gardens*, Refinery29, *EatingWell*, and more. Her work is informed by two decades of study, certification, and international teaching in the art and practice of meditation, yoga, and psychosomatic therapies. She is a devoted co-conspirator to organizations decolonizing food and wellness for all.

Lily was educated at Yale University and lives in Maui, Hawaiʻi, where she grew up, on occupied native Hawaiian land.

REBECCA WALKER has contributed to the global conversation about race, gender, power, and the evolution of the human family for three decades. Since graduating from Yale, she has authored seven bestselling books on subjects ranging from intergenerational feminism and multiracial identity to Black Cool and ambivalent motherhood, and written dozens of articles on topics as varied as Barack Obama's masculinity, the work of visual artist Ana Mendieta, and the changing configuration of the American family.

Rebecca has written, developed, and produced film and television projects with Warner Brothers, NBC, Amazon, HBO, and Paramount, and spoken at over four hundred universities and corporate campuses internationally, including Harvard, Out and Equal, Museum of the African Diaspora, and TEDx Lund. When Rebecca was 21, she co-founded the Third Wave Fund, which makes grants to womxn and transgender youth working for social justice. She was named by *Time* magazine as one of the most influential leaders of her generation—and continues to teach her masterclass, The Art of Memoir, at gorgeous and inspiring places around the world.

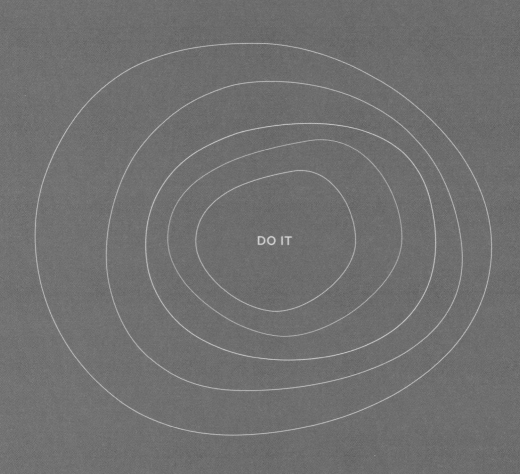